MW00904576

Dedication:

This book is dedicated to my beautiful friend Avery and her incredible parents, Joe and Lisa. Your family continues to be such an inspiration for people to understand and appreciate all the different aspects life has to offer. Avery has taught children, teachers, and parents about Down syndrome, as well as how to show empathy and compassion to all.

ACKNOWLEDGMENTS

Kyah, I'm so excited for the world to see what an amazing artist you are at eleven years old. Thank you for illustrating my books.
Thank you to my editor Molly for helping me find the right words.
Alyssa, you are an amazing photographer and I appreciate you taking the pictures.
Terha, you are a wonderful mentor, motivator, and without you this book would not have happened, thank you.
Sonja, thank you for all of your designing skills for this book.
I appreciate your expertise Dr. Ralph and guided path to publishing this book.
Thank you Anthony for assembling, editing, and helping to make this book so beautiful.
Thank you to my parents for always supporting me and encouraging me to follow my passion.
Most of all, thank you to my wonderful husband and children for being patient and always supporting my adventures.

I love you all.

Hi! My name is Avery. Are you as nervous about starting school as I am? That's okay, we will get through this together. It might make things a little less scary if we have a friend by our side. Don't you agree? Okay, let's be friends.

Making friends can be difficult for me because I don't talk the way you do. I use my body, facial expressions, and I might make sounds to let you know that I'm happy or upset.

We might not have the same interests, but I bet you can think of something we both like to do. Once you get to know me, we could be the best of friends.

If we are playing together and I'm doing something that you don't like, please just ask me or help to stop. I may be nervous about something and I don't realize what I'm doing. Some people bite their nails or pick their nose; I sometimes rock back and forth, make silly noises, or wiggle things to calm my mind and body. Do you like to sing? Me too. If you see me having a hard time, maybe you could sing me your favorite song. I'd really like that.

To be my friend, I ask that you accept me and my uniqueness, as I will accept yours. I may need help sometimes when things get difficult for me, but what I need most of all, let's have fun and laugh a lot. I love to have a good time just like you do.

Ho

Ha

He

I bet you're wondering if we have anything in common. Well, I already know the answer, and the answer is yes! I love to travel with my family, listen to music, and my favorite thing to do is swimming.

Do you know how to swim?
If not, that's okay, I can help teach you.

Sometimes, I get very involved in my play and even though I may seem like I want to play alone, I really don't. I would love it if you would come up to me, hold out your hand, and say, "Avery, let's play."

My days are probably quite a bit busier than yours. During school, I have lots of special teachers who help me to understand things that are more challenging for me to learn. If you see me leave the room with another adult, don't worry, I'll be back soon.

I also have several therapies each week after school to help me build my muscles, be more independent, and make good choices. Yes, I have a full schedule, but it's all worthwhile because it helps me to be more independent.

Even with a busy schedule, my mom and dad always make sure we have time to go on adventures because I love to see new things. Maybe our families could go together on an adventure sometime; I'd really like that.

School can be hard for me because it feels like I have super powers with my hearing, smelling, seeing, feeling, and tasting. So yes, I'm kind of like a super hero.

More than likely, the everyday sounds you hear are very loud for me, so don't be alarmed if you see me covering my ears. If you hear another student making a loud noise, please ask them to stop.

Smells are stronger for me than they might be for you. Don't let it hurt your feelings if I go sit somewhere else at lunch, the smells might be too strong for me.

The lights in the classroom are brighter for me and often hurt my eyes. Sometimes, I wear these really cool glasses that help make the lights not so bright. Have you ever looked up at the sun? Ouch, right?

Sometimes, I feel like everyone is staring at me when I am doing something that helps me to calm my body or mind. I don't like that.

Would you like it if everyone stared at you while you were struggling? I didn't think so. Distraction helps me to forget my worries and think about something positive. Maybe you could read me a book.
I would really like that.

I don't like to get upset at school; I bet you don't either. I don't like to do things that are hard for me. Learning a new skill takes patience, focus, and the ability to sit for long periods of time.

All of these things are hard. Don't you agree? Sometimes, a friend is all I need. I may not use my words to tell you thank you, but know when I smile at you, that means 'thank you' in my language.

Please understand that words are not the only way to communicate. I use my eyes, eyebrows, mouth, body, hands, noises, and so much more to tell people how I feel. Without using your words, how can you show me how you fell?

It really bothers me when people talk about me as if I'm not standing right there. I really wish they would talk to me. I can hear them and I understand what they are saying, I just don't have a way to let them know that I understand everything they are saying about me. Imagine living in a world where you understand the language, but nobody understands your language.

Let's play a game. Try to communicate with me without using any language from your mouth. You can only use facial expressions and gestures like pointing while we play. I bet you'll be surprised at how well your body and face can communicate with me.

If I am having a hard day, please don't stare at me. It makes me feel uncomfortable and embarrassed. Instead, ask me, my teacher, or my parents questions. If I see you're having a hard day, I will try to help you because that's what friends are for.

You may not understand why I do some things, so let me help you understand. I love to pour water onto the palm of my hand. The soft water splashing my hand makes it tickle and makes me giggle. If you haven't done it, you should give it a try. I also love to spin and spin, but unlike you, I normally don't get dizzy. It just gives me a tickle in my tummy.

Please have patience, as I try to figure out your complicated world. Everyone needs to feel a connection and to feel like they belong to their class. How great would it be if we could be that connection to each other?

We all have the same emotions. I feel happy, sad, excited, and mad just like you. Each of us expresses our emotions differently and that's okay because that's what makes us unique from each other. When I'm mad, I may grunt, turn my back to you, or throw something. When I am happy, I will smile, giggle, or hug you. We are alike in that our faces show how we feel.

We all have special things about us that makes us different from one another. I'll teach you something about me. I'm unique from you because I have Down syndrome.
That means that when I was growing in my mommy's tummy, I grew differently than you. My brain and body grew differently than yours did, but our hearts, the love for our family, and how we enjoy playing and making friends are the same. I can't wait to spend this school year getting to know each other.